HOW TO PRAY

How to Pray

A Step-by-Step Guide to
Prayer in Islam

MUSTAFA UMAR

ISBN-13: 978-1463578909
ISBN-10: 1463578903

www.welcometoislam.co

Printed in the United States of America

In the Name of God
The Most Kind and Merciful

CONTENTS

Introduction

There has been an urgent need for a simple and concise guide which teaches the basics of prayer for Muslims. This book has been designed for people who don't know how to pray yet or those who aren't sure whether they learned correctly.

Since you have chosen Islam as your way of life, you probably are eager to start learning as much as you can. Islam is not only theory but practice as well. There can be no true belief without action. Prayer is the first and most important step in the path of Islam. A Muslim must pray to God five times a day. It's the Islamic spiritual diet. Just like we eat several times throughout the day to keep our body healthy, we must connect with our Lord throughout the day to keep our soul healthy. Prayer cleans our sins, as if we are taking a bath five times a day to clean our body. But in Islam, the soul is more important than the body. The prayer removes any arrogance from our ego and puts us in our true place as servants of God. Each prayer usually takes only about 5 to 10 minutes, so it's not really difficult, although it can take some getting used to.

Prayer should be taken very seriously because it is the first thing a Muslim will be questioned about on the Day of Judgment. After belief in the unity of God, nothing is more important than prayer. All the prophets, throughout history, performed some form of prayer. It was the foundation from which they drew their strength to call others to the way of God. The prayer, if learned and practiced correctly, can be an infinite source of strength and relief for you as well in your life.

In this book you will learn the prayers by reading and observing the diagrams with clear and simple descriptions of what to do. Please note that there are slight variations in the way different Muslims pray: both in words and actions of the prayer. This is due to different ways of interpreting the primary texts of Islam: the Qur'an and the Sunnah. If you notice these differences or if someone points them out to you don't pay much attention to them for now. In time, you will learn to appreciate these differences of opinion as you increase in knowledge.

Remember, prayer takes some time to learn, so take it slow and steady.

Chapter 1: Before You Pray

There are some prerequisites that must be done before prayer, so you will learn them before learning how to pray.

WUDŪ'

Before praying, you must wash certain parts of your body so you are in a state of purity before you stand in front of God. This is called wudū', or ablution. This is how it's done:

Hands

Go to a sink, turn on the water, and wash both of your hands up to your wrists.

Mouth

Then, cup your right hand and fill it with water. Take that water into your mouth, swirl it around, and then spit it out. Do this three times.

Nose

Then, cup your right hand again, fill it with water, and sniff it into your nose. Be careful not to hurt yourself by sniffing too quickly. Clean the inside of your nose and blow the water out. Do this three times.

Face

 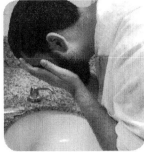

Now cup both of your hands and fill them with water. Close your eyes, bring the water to your face, and wash your entire face. Do this three times.

Arms

Now wash your right arm from your fingertips all the way up to the elbow. Do this three times. Now do the same for your left arm three times.

Head

Now, wet both your hands and wipe over your head.

Ears

With the water left on your hands, insert your index fingers into your ears and clean the inside with the index fingers and the back of your ears with the thumbs.

Feet

Lastly, remove your shoes and socks, and put your foot in the sink. Wash your right foot up to the ankle three times. Then wash your left foot three times. You have now completed your wudū' and are ready to pray.

It is not necessary to perform wudū' for every prayer. If anything comes out of your private parts [like urine, excrement, or gas] or if you go to sleep, you must renew your wudū' again.

If you have intercourse, or even a wet dream, you must shower and wash your entire body in order to get into a state of purity for prayer.

Menstruating women should not perform the five daily prayers during their period. The same applies to women during their post-natal bleeding period after giving birth. This is a mercy from God because of their condition and they don't even need to make up the prayers later. However, they should remember God in their heart throughout the day and continue to learn more about Islam.

CLEANLINESS

Before praying, you must make sure that your clothes, your body, and the place where you will pray are clean. If there is some dirt on the floor or sweat on your clothes, it is ok, as long as there are no impurities. The following things are impure in Islam and you should make sure to clean them off before starting your prayer: blood, vomit, urine, and feces. You only need to wash this impurity off with water if you don't have soap available.

DRESS CODE

Before praying, you must make sure that you are dressed properly, just like you dress properly before meeting a dignitary or person of authority. The dress code for prayer is the same as the Islamic dress code when in public. Even if you are praying where no one else can see you, you still cover out of respect for God. Since men and women are created physically different, their dress code differs.

Men are required to cover from their navel to their knees, at minimum. They should not pray in their underwear or in extremely revealing shorts. Women are required to cover their entire body with the exception of their face, hands, and feet. To do this, a woman will usually wear any type of loose fitting clothing like a long skirt and a top and then cover her hair and neck with a headscarf. These clothes should not be tight and revealing.

TIMINGS

The five prayers are spread throughout the day, so you are always remembering God. To make life easy for us, God has given a span of time in which we can offer our prayers conveniently. Each prayer takes about 5-10 minutes and each span of time is usually an hour or more . Prayer timings depend on the position of the sun,[1] so they change every day and vary from place to place. To find out the prayer times in your area get a prayer calendar from your local mosque or go to www.islamicfinder.com. Type in your zip code and click 'go'. On the right column of the webpage, you will see a table that looks like the following:

Today's Prayer Time	
Day	Thursday
Fajr	5:21
Sunrise	6:29
Dhuhr	12:07
Asr	3:19
Maghrib	5:45
Isha	6:54

Let's go over this table as an example. The first prayer of the day is called Fajr and begins at 5:21AM. This prayer ends at sunrise which is at 6:29AM. This means you can pray the Fajr prayer anytime between these two times. The second prayer of the day is Ẓuhr [also spelled Dhuhr], and begins at 12:07PM. This prayer ends before the next one starts at 3:19PM. So you can pray the Ẓuhr prayer anytime between 12:07PM and 3:19PM. The third prayer of the

---

1   This used to be the way people determined time before watches were invented.

day is Asr, which is between 3:19PM and 5:45PM. The fourth prayer, Maghrib, begins at sunset, which is at 5:45PM and lasts until 6:54PM. The final prayer is Isha and begins at 6:54PM and lasts until 5:21AM of the next day, just before Fajr. Try to memorize the names of these prayers if you can because they are used by all Muslims. It is strongly recommended that you pray each prayer as early as possible and not delay unnecessarily. Being lazy in observing prayer on time reflects your attitude towards God. Try to never miss a single prayer. In case you do, make it up, with a feeling of regret, as soon as you are able to do so, even if the time has passed.

DIRECTION OF PRAYER

Prayer can be performed anywhere: in a park, a shopping center, a parking lot, etc. When praying, all Muslims in the world face toward the direction of the city of Makkah in Arabia. This unites all Muslims around the world. To find out the direction, go to www.qiblalocator.com and type in your zip code. A red line will show you which direction you should face. Either figure out the direction through the map or use a compass to determine the location. This will be the direction you always face, so you only need to check once for each location. This direction is called the 'qiblah' in Arabic and you should calculate it for your home, school, or work.

Chapter 2: How to Pray

Phase 1

Now that you know how to prepare for prayer, you are ready to learn the motions and what to say, so you can follow the way that Prophet Muhammad taught us to pray. Prayer should be done in Arabic, because that is the original language of the Qur'an. Don't worry; you don't need to learn a whole new language. You can just memorize some Arabic phrases that you need in order to perform the prayer and learn what they mean.

Prayer takes some time to learn, so we have developed a three phase process to make it easy for you. No one is expected to learn the entire prayer in one day. Therefore, each successive phase will build on the previous one and you will learn gradually.

Throughout the prayer, you will be standing, bowing, sitting, and prostrating. Each position has a physical posture as well as a spiritual meaning. In phase 1, we will only focus on how to perform these stances and learn a few Arabic phrases for now.

THE PRAYER MOTIONS AND STANCES

Read the description of each position, look at the picture, and try to practice doing it yourself. Ask another practicing Muslim to help you if needed.

Standing

Front   Side

Stand facing towards Makkah. Keep your hands to your sides. Your feet should be about shoulder width apart. Your eyes should be focused[2] on the ground a few feet in front of you.

This is the stance of a person at full attention who is focused.

---

2   Remember, during the prayer, you may close your eyes for concentration whenever you want.

Raising Hands

Front   Side

Begin the prayer by raising your hands near your ears. Make sure your palms are facing forward.

This signifies that you are leaving all other thoughts in your mind behind as you begin connecting with God.

Standing for Recitation

Front   Side

Use your right hand to grab your left hand at the wrist. Place both hands on your body above your navel.

This is a stance of humility which shows your awe and respect in front of God.

Bowing

Front   Side

Bend down and grab your knees. Keep your fingers slightly spread apart. Your eyes should be focused where your feet are. Try to keep your back straight as much as possible.

This is a stance of humbling the body before God by lowering it in a bowing position. It reminds us of our place in front of God.

Prostration

Slowly get down on your knees. Place your hands on the ground in front of you. Put your forehead and nose on the ground between your hands. Keep your hands flat on the ground near your ears with your fingers together and facing forward. Make sure your elbows are off the ground.

You should be standing on your toes with the rest of your feet off the ground.

Front

Side

This is a stance of the utmost humility where you put your face, which represents your honor, on the floor in front of God.

Back (Feet)

Side (Feet)

Sitting

Sit on the floor with your hands on your thighs near the knees. Keep your fingers together. If you are able to, sit on your left foot while standing on the toes of your right foot which is a little out to the side. If this position is difficult, sit in any comfortable way.

Front

Side

This is supposed to be a comfortable and relaxing position which gives you a break after having stood for a while.

Back (Feet)

Side (Pointing)

Finish the Prayer

Right Salam

Left Salam

Conclude the prayer by moving your head to the right

while looking over your right shoulder. Then move your head to the left in the same way.

While moving your head right and left, you will also learn to say a greeting of peace. It means that you are praying for all the people around you.

WHAT TO SAY DURING PRAYER

We will now learn what to say during the prayer. These are the Arabic phrases that we will use:

ARABIC	ENGLISH
al-lā-hu ak-bar	*God is the greatest*
al-ham-du lil-lāh	*Praise is due to God*
sa-mi-al lā-hu li-man ḥa-mi-dah	*God has heard the one who praised Him*
as-salāmu ʿalaykum wa raḥmatullah	*May the peace and mercy of God be with you*

Try to memorize these Arabic phrases before beginning the prayer. You will say each of them either silently in your mind or whisper them to yourself. If possible, have some-one experienced help you pronounce them. Don't worry about pronouncing them perfectly for now. That will come with time.

PERFORMING THE PRAYERS: STEP-BY-STEP

Now that you know the movements of prayer and are familiar with the Arabic, let's begin the prayer. Prayer consists of a number of units, or cycles, where you repeat much of what you do and say in each unit. There are three different types: a two-unit, three-unit, and four-unit prayer. The five daily prayers consist of all three types, so you will need to learn all of them. Remember the posture for each stance and follow along.

A TWO-UNIT PRAYER

1.1 Standing

Start in standing position.

1.2 Raising Hands

Begin the prayer by raising your hands while saying: "al-lā-hu ak-bar"

1.3 Standing for Recitation

After placing your hands say: "al-ham-du lil-lāh" three times

1.4 Bowing

Go into bowing position while saying: "al-lā-hu ak-bar"

Then say: "al-ham-du lil-lāh" three times

1.5 Intermediate Standing

Return to standing position while saying: "sa-mi-al lā-hu li-man ḥa-mi-dah"

1.6 Prostration

Go into prostration while saying: "al-lā-hu ak-bar"

Then say: "al-ham-du lil-lāh" three times

1.7 Intermediate Sitting

Rise up into sitting position while saying: "al-lā-hu ak-bar"

1.8 Prostration #2

Go into prostration again while saying: "al-lā-hu ak-bar"

Then say: "al-ham-du lil-lāh" three times

2.1 Standing

Return to 'standing for recitation' position while saying: "al-lā-hu ak-bar"

This completes one unit of prayer. You are now in the second unit.

Then say: "al-ham-du lil-lāh" three times

2.2 Bowing

Go into bowing position while saying: "al-lā-hu ak-bar"

Then say: "al-ham-du lil-lāh" three times

2.3 Intermediate Standing

Return to standing position while saying: "sa-mi-al lā-hu li-man ḥa-mi-dah"

2.4 Prostration

Go into prostration while saying: "al-lā-hu ak-bar"

Then say: "al-ham-du lil-lāh" three times

2.5 Intermediate Sitting

Rise up into sitting position while saying: "al-lā-hu ak-bar"

2.6 Prostration #2

Go into prostration while saying: "al-lā-hu ak-bar"

Then say: "al-ham-du lil-lāh" three times

2.7 Sitting

Rise up into sitting position while saying: "al-lā-hu ak-bar"

Then say: "al-ham-du lil-lāh" three times

2.8 Finish the Prayer

Conclude the prayer by moving your head to the right and say "as-salāmu 'alaykum wa raḥmatullah". Then move your head to the left and say the same thing.

A THREE-UNIT PRAYER

Now that you are able to perform a two unit prayer, you can easily add one more unit and perform a three unit prayer. The only difference is that you will be in sitting position twice. This is how it's done:

1.1 Standing

Start in standing position.

1.2 Raising Hands

Begin the prayer by raising your hands while saying: "al-lā-hu ak-bar"

1.3 Standing for Recitation

After placing your hands say: "al-ham-du lil-lāh" three times

1.4 Bowing

Go into bowing position while saying: "al-lā-hu ak-bar"

Then say: "al-ham-du lil-lāh" three times

1.5 Intermediate Standing

Return to standing position while saying: "sa-mi-al lā-hu li-man ḥa-mi-dah"

1.6 Prostration

Go into prostration while saying: "al-lā-hu ak-bar"

Then say: "al-ham-du lil-lāh" three times

1.7 Intermediate Sitting

Rise up into sitting position while saying: "al-lā-hu ak-bar"

1.8 Prostration #2

Go into prostration again while saying: "al-lā-hu ak-bar"

Then say: "al-ham-du lil-lāh" three times

2.1 Standing

Return to 'standing for recitation' position while saying: "al-lā-hu ak-bar"

This completes one unit of prayer. You are now in the second unit.

Then say: "al-ham-du lil-lāh" three times

2.2 Bowing

Go into bowing position while saying: "al-lā-hu ak-bar"

Then say: "al-ham-du lil-lāh" three times

2.3 Intermediate Standing

Return to standing position while saying: "sa-mi-al lā-hu li-man ha-mi-dah"

2.4 Prostration

Go into prostration while saying: "al-lā-hu ak-bar"

Then say: "al-ham-du lil-lāh" three times

2.5 Intermediate Sitting

Rise up into sitting position while saying: "al-lā-hu ak-bar"

2.6 Prostration #2

Go into prostration while saying: "al-lā-hu ak-bar"

Then say: "al-ham-du lil-lāh" three times

2.7 Sitting

Say "al-lā-hu ak-bar" and rise up into sitting position.

Say: "al-ham-du lil-lāh" three times.

3.1 Standing

Say "al-lā-hu ak-bar" and return to standing position with hands folded. This completes two units of prayer. You are now in the third unit.

3.2 Standing for Recitation

After placing your hands say: "al-ham-du lil-lāh" three times

3.3 Bowing

Go into bowing position while saying: "al-lā-hu ak-bar"

Then say: "al-ham-du lil-lāh" three times

3.4 Intermediate Standing

Return to standing position while saying: "sa-mi-al lā-hu li-man ḥa-mi-dah"

3.5 Prostration

Go into prostration while saying: "al-lā-hu ak-bar"

Then say: "al-ham-du lil-lāh" three times

3.6 Intermediate Sitting

Rise up into sitting position while saying: "al-lā-hu ak-bar"

3.7 Prostration #2

Go into prostration again while saying: "al-lā-hu ak-bar"

Then say: "al-ham-du lil-lāh" three times

3.8 Sitting

Rise up into sitting position while saying: "al-lā-hu ak-bar"

Then say: "al-ham-du lil-lāh" three times

3.9 Finish the Prayer

Conclude the prayer by moving your head to the right and say "as-salāmu 'alaykum wa raḥmatullah". Then move your head to the left and say the same thing.

A FOUR-UNIT PRAYER: STEP-BY-STEP

Now that you are able to perform a three unit prayer, you can easily add one more unit and perform a four unit prayer. In this prayer you will be in sitting position twice. This is how it's done:

1.1 Standing

Start in standing position.

1.2 Raising Hands

Begin the prayer by raising your hands while saying: "al-lā-hu ak-bar"

1.3 Standing for Recitation

After placing your hands say: "al-ham-du lil-lāh" three times

1.4 Bowing

Go into bowing position while saying: "al-lā-hu ak-bar"

Then say: "al-ham-du lil-lāh" three times

1.5 Intermediate Standing

Return to standing position while saying: "sa-mi-al lā-hu li-man ḥa-mi-dah"

1.6 Prostration

Go into prostration while saying: "al-lā-hu ak-bar"

Then say: "al-ham-du lil-lāh" three times

1.7 Intermediate Sitting

Rise up into sitting position while saying: "al-lā-hu ak-bar"

1.8 Prostration #2

Go into prostration again while saying: "al-lā-hu ak-bar"

Then say: "al-ham-du lil-lāh" three times

2.1 Standing

Return to 'standing for recitation' position while saying: "al-lā-hu ak-bar"

This completes one unit of prayer. You are now in the second unit.

Then say: "al-ham-du lil-lāh" three times

2.2 Bowing

Go into bowing position while saying: "al-lā-hu ak-bar"

Then say: "al-ham-du lil-lāh" three times

2.3 Intermediate Standing

Return to standing position while saying: "sa-mi-al lā-hu li-man ḥa-mi-dah"

2.4 Prostration

Go into prostration while saying: "al-lā-hu ak-bar"

Then say: "al-ham-du lil-lāh" three times

2.5 Intermediate Sitting

Rise up into sitting position while saying: "al-lā-hu ak-bar"

2.6 Prostration #2

Go into prostration while saying: "al-lā-hu ak-bar"

Then say: "al-ham-du lil-lāh" three times

2.7 Sitting

Say "al-lā-hu ak-bar" and rise up into sitting position.

Say: "al-ham-du lil-lāh" three times.

3.1 Standing

Say "al-lā-hu ak-bar" and return to standing position with hands folded. This completes two units of prayer. You are now in the third unit.

3.2 Standing for Recitation

After placing your hands say: "al-ham-du lil-lāh" three times

3.3 Bowing

Go into bowing position while saying: "al-lā-hu ak-bar"

Then say: "al-ham-du lil-lāh" three times

3.4 Intermediate Standing

Return to standing position while saying: "sa-mi-al lā-hu li-man ha-mi-dah"

3.5 Prostration

Go into prostration while saying: "al-lā-hu ak-bar"

Then say: "al-ham-du lil-lāh" three times

3.6 Intermediate Sitting

Rise up into sitting position while saying: "al-lā-hu ak-bar"

3.7 Prostration #2

Go into prostration again while saying: "al-lā-hu ak-bar"

Then say: "al-ham-du lil-lāh" three times

4.1 Standing

Say "al-lā-hu ak-bar" and return to standing position with hands folded. This completes two units of prayer. You are now in the third unit.

4.2 Standing for Recitation

After placing your hands say: "al-ham-du lil-lāh" three times

4.3 Bowing

Go into bowing position while saying: "al-lā-hu ak-bar"

Then say: "al-ham-du lil-lāh" three times

4.4 Intermediate Standing

Return to standing position while saying: "sa-mi-al lā-hu li-man ḥa-mi-dah"

4.5 Prostration

Go into prostration while saying: "al-lā-hu ak-bar"

Then say: "al-ham-du lil-lāh" three times

4.6 Intermediate Sitting

Rise up into sitting position while saying: "al-lā-hu ak-bar"

4.7 Prostration #2

Go into prostration again while saying: "al-lā-hu ak-bar"

Then say: "al-ham-du lil-lāh" three times

4.8 Sitting

Rise up into sitting position while saying: "al-lā-hu ak-bar"

Then say: "al-ham-du lil-lāh" three times

4.9 Finish the Prayer

Conclude the prayer by moving your head to the right and say "as-salāmu 'alaykum wa raḥmatullah". Then move your head to the left and say the same thing.

START PRACTICING

Now that you know how to perform all three types of prayers, it's time to start practicing. Since you already know how to determine the timings of each of the five prayers, you only need to learn how many units are in each prayer:

- Fajr ("Dawn Prayer") consists of two units
- Ẓuhr ("Afternoon Prayer") consists of four units
- 'Asr ("Late Afternoon Prayer") consists of four units
- Maghrib ("Evening Prayer") consists of three units
- 'Ishā' ("Night Prayer") consists of four units

That's it. Now you can start praying all five prayers. Pray this way until you are ready to move to Phase 2. Remember that prayer is a time for contemplation and spiritual advancement. Try not to get distracted or make any unnecessary movements. Every part of you should be involved in the prayer: body, mind, and soul.

Chapter 3: How to Pray

Phase 2

Now that you know how to go through the motions of the prayer, we will learn some more Arabic phrases which glorify and praise God. Up until now, we have been substituting the phrase 'al-ham-du lil'lāh' for other longer Arabic phrases so you didn't need to memorize as much.

These are the new Arabic phrases that we will use in the prayer:

ARABIC	ENGLISH
bis-mil lā-hir rah-mā-nir ra-hīm	*In the name of God, the Most Kind and Merciful*
sub-hā-na rab-bī-yal a-ẓīm	*Glory be to my Lord, the great*
rab-ba-nā la-kal hamd	*Our Lord, you are deserving of praise*
sub-hā-na rab-bī-yal a-lā	*Glory be to my Lord, the highest*

ash-ha-du al-lā ilā-ha ill-lal-lāh wa ash-ha-du an-na mu-ham-ma-dan ab-du-hu wa ra-sū-lu-hu	*I declare that no one deserves to be worshipped except God and I declare that Muhammad is His servant and messenger.*

Try to memorize these Arabic phrases before beginning.

MODIFICATIONS IN EACH STEP OF THE PRAYER

Notice the changes in the following steps of the prayer:

Start the Prayer

No changes.

Standing

NEW Say: "bis-mil lā-hir rah-mā-nir ra-hīm"

Say: "al-ham-du lil-lāh" three times.

Bowing

Say "al-lā-hu ak-bar" while going into bowing position.

NEW Say: "sub-hā-na rab-bī-yal a-ẓīm" three times.

Intermediate Standing

Say "sa-mi-al lā-hu li-man ḥa-mi-dah" while standing up.

NEW Say: "rab-ba-nā la-kal hamd"

Prostration

Say "al-lā-hu ak-bar" and go into prostration.

NEW Say: "sub-hā-na rab-bī-yal a-lā" three times.

Intermediate Sitting

No changes.

Prostration #2

Say "al-lā-hu ak-bar" and go into prostration again.

NEW Say: "sub-hā-na rab-bī-yal a-lā" three times.

Sitting

Say "al-lā-hu ak-bar" and rise up into sitting position.

Say: "al-ham-du lil-lāh" three times.

NEW Say: "ash-ha-du al-lā ilā-ha ill-lal-lāh wa ash-ha-du an-na mu-ham-ma-dan ab-du-hu wa ra-sū-lu-hu" and point forward with your index finger while saying it.

Finish the Prayer

No changes.

START PRACTICING

Now that you have learned new phrases which are either added or substituted for another phrase, you can start praying in this way. Pray this way until you are ready to move to Phase 3.

Chapter 4: How to Pray

Phase 3

Now that you have learnt some more Arabic phrases we will learn the rest of what to say in the prayer.

These are the new Arabic phrases that we will use in the prayer:

ARABIC	ENGLISH
a-ū-dhu bil-lā-hi mi-nash shay-ṭā-nir ra-jīm	*I seek protection with God from the cursed Satan*
al-ḥam-du lil-lā-hi rab-bil ā-la-mīn. ar-raḥ-mā-nir ra-ḥīm. mā-li-ki yaw-mid dīn. iy-yā-ka na-bu-du wa iy-yā-ka nas-ta-īn. ih-di-naṣ ṣi-rā-tal mus-ta-qīm. si-rā-tal la-dhī-na an-am-ta a-lay-him, ghay-ril magh-ḍū-bi a-lay-him wa laḍ ḍāllīn.	*Praise belongs to God, Lord of the Worlds. The Most Kind and Merciful. Master of the Day of Judgment. It is you we worship; it is you we ask for help. Guide us on the straight path: the path of those you have blessed, those who incur no anger and who have not gone astray.*
ā-mīn	*Please answer [this prayer]*

qul hu-wal- lā-hu a-ḥad. al-lā-huṣ ṣa-mad. lam ya-lid wa lam yū-lad. wa lam ya-kul-la-hu ku-fu-wan a-ḥad.	*Say, He is God, the one. God, the eternal. He neither gives birth nor was given birth to. No one is comparable to Him.*
at-ta-ḥī-yā-tu lil-lā-hi waṣ-ṣa-la-wā-tu waṭ-ṭay-yi-bā-tu as-sa-lā-mu a-lay-ka ay-yu-han na-bī-yu wa raḥ-ma-tul-lā-hi wa ba-ra-kā-tu-hu as-sa-lā-mu a-lay-nā wa a-lā i-bā-dil-lā-hiṣ ṣā-li-hīn	*Greetings, prayers, and all pure things ultimately belong to God. May the peace of God be with you, Prophet, as well as God's mercy and blessings. May the peace of God be with us and with all of God's righteous servants.*
al-lā-hum-ma ṣal-li a-lā mu-ham-ma-diw wa a-lā ā-li mu-ham-ma-din ka-mā ṣal-lay-ta a-lā ib-rā-hī-ma wa a-lā ā-li ib-rā-hī-ma in-na-ka ḥa-mī-dum ma-jīd. al-lā-hum-ma bā-rik a-lā mu-ham-ma-diw wa a-lā ā-li mu-ham-ma-din ka-mā bā-rak-ta a-lā ib-rā-hī-ma wa a-lā ā-li ib-rā-hī-ma in-na-ka ḥa-mī-dum ma-jīd	*God, bless Muhammad and his family, just as you have blessed Ibrāhīm and his family. You are the praiseworthy and glorious. God, favor Muhammad and his family, just as you have favored Ibrāhīm and his family. You are the praiseworthy and glorious.*

Try to memorize these Arabic phrases before beginning.

MODIFICATIONS IN EACH STEP OF THE PRAYER

Notice the changes in the following steps of the prayer:

Start the Prayer

No changes.

41

Standing

NEW Say: "a-ū-dhu bil-lā-hi mi-nash shay-ṭā-nir ra-jīm"

Say: "bis-mil lā-hir rah-mā-nir ra-hīm"

NEW Say: "al-ḥam-du lil-lā-hi rab-bil ā-la-mīn. ar-raḥ-mā-nir ra-ḥīm. mā-li-ki yaw-mid dīn. iy-yā-ka na-bu-du wa iy-yā-ka nas-ta-īn. ih-di-naṣ ṣi-rā-tal mus-ta-qīm. si-rā-tal la-dhī-na an-am-ta a-lay-him, ghay-ril magh-ḍū-bi a-lay-him wa laḍ ḍāllīn."

NEW Say: "ā-mīn"

NEW Say [only in the first and second unit of prayer]: qul hu-wal- lā-hu a-ḥad. al-lā-huṣ ṣa-mad. lam ya-lid wa lam yū-lad. wa lam ya-kul-la-hu ku-fu-wan a-ḥad.

Bowing

No changes.

Intermediate Standing

No changes.

Prostration

No changes.

Intermediate Sitting

No changes.

Prostration #2

No changes.

Sitting

Say "al-lā-hu ak-bar" and rise up into sitting position.

NEW Say: "at-ta-ḥī-yā-tu lil-lā-hi waṣ-ṣa-la-wā-tu waṭ-ṭay-yi-bā-tu as-sa-lā-mu a-lay-ka ay-yu-han na-bī-yu wa raḥ-ma-tul-lā-hi wa ba-ra-kā-tu-hu as-sa-lā-mu a-lay-nā wa a-lā i-bā-dil-lā-hiṣ ṣā-li-hīn"

Say: "ash-ha-du al-lā ilā-ha ill-lal-lāh wa ash-ha-du an-na mu-ham-ma-dan ab-du-hu wa ra-sū-lu-hu" and point forward with your index finger while saying it.

NEW Say: "al-lā-hum-ma ṣal-li a-lā mu-ḥam-ma-diw wa a-lā ā-li mu-ḥam-ma-din ka-mā ṣal-lay-ta a-lā ib-rā-hī-ma wa a-lā ā-li ib-rā-hī-ma in-na-ka ḥa-mī-dum ma-jīd. al-lā-hum-ma bā-rik a-lā mu-ḥam-ma-diw wa a-lā ā-li mu-ḥam-ma-din ka-mā bā-rak-ta a-lā ib-rā-hī-ma wa a-lā ā-li ib-rā-hī-ma in-na-ka ḥa-mī-dum ma-jīd"

Finish the Prayer

No changes.

WHEN YOU FORGET

There are quite a few Arabic phrases to memorize. If at any time during the prayer you cannot remember what to say, just say 'al-lā-hu ak-bar' or 'al-ham-du lil-lāh' as a substitute, and continue the prayer.

Chapter 5: Group Prayer

Prayers should be performed in a group, or congregation, whenever possible. When praying in a group, one person will be chosen to lead the prayer and will stand in front. The rest of the people following will form a line behind him. If there are women, they will form a line behind the line of men for reasons of modesty.

The prayer leader, also known as the 'imām', will say the following parts of the prayer out loud:

- Every 'allāhu akbar'

- "sami'allahu liman ḥamidah"

- "as-salāmu 'alaykum wa raḥmatullah"

The rest of the prayer will be either said silently in your mind or whispered to yourself. Everyone will follow the leader in the movements of the prayer.

During the Fajr, Maghrib, and 'Ishā' prayers, the prayer leader will also recite the verses from the Qur'an out loud while standing in the first two units of each prayer. This is due to the fact that most people don't work during these hours and the group is larger. The people behind him will listen attentively to the verses being recited.

Chapter 6: Friday Prayer

I t is obvious that you will not be able to make it to the mosque for all five prayers every day. Perhaps you may not find another Muslim to pray with throughout most of the week. However, it is very important to meet and pray with other Muslims. This is why Islam has set a special prayer on Friday afternoon, when all Muslims are required to attend the mosque, listen to a motivating sermon, pray, and get to know other Muslims. All adult Muslim men must take time off from their work and attend this prayer if there is a mosque nearby. Women and young children are excused if they are busy, but they should try to attend at least sometimes. It is unfortunate that Friday is not a holiday, but you have a legal right in most countries to take off an hour or so for religious reasons.

Friday prayer, or 'Ju-mu-ah', is exactly like the two units of Fajr prayer, read aloud, except that it is prayed at Zuhr time and must be in a group. If you make this prayer, it substitutes for Zuhr prayer. However, if you miss the prayer, you must pray four units of Zuhr as usual.

Chapter 7: Additional Daily Prayers

SUNNAH PRAYERS

There are other prayers connected to the five daily prayers. Though they are not required, there is great reward in performing them and a Muslim should try to get into the habit of praying these prayers as well. These prayers are said individually and in a low voice, either before or after the five prayers.

These voluntary additional prayers are usually called Sunnah prayers while the mandatory five prayers are called Farḍ prayers. The only major difference between the two is that in a Farḍ prayer, only al-Fātiḥah is recited in the third and fourth unit, while in the Sunnah prayers, other verses must be recited, just like in the first two units of prayer.

Below is a table which shows how many units are in each prayer:

PRAYER	SUNNAH BEFORE	FARD	SUNNAH AFTER
Fajr	2	2	–
Zuhr	4	4	2
'Asr	–	4	–
Maghrib	–	3	2
'Ishā'	–	4	2

WITR PRAYER

There is another highly recommended prayer called 'witr' which should be prayed after 'Ishā' and before the time of Fajr comes in. This prayer is beyond the scope of this book, but you should try to learn it if possible.

Chapter 8: Meanings Behind the Prayer

Now we will go over the meaning behind each action and statement in the prayer so that it goes beyond being a formulaic ritual and becomes a way to really connect with God.

The more you learn to focus and understand the prayer the more you will develop so that you restrain yourself from immoral behavior. The prayer will then be able to function as an infinite source of strength in all aspects of your life and can even be the best way to deal with stress and challenges in life.

BEFORE YOU PRAY

You perform wudū' as a symbolic gesture of spiritually cleansing yourself before you stand in front of God.

You clean your clothes, body, and place of prayer which represents the bare minimum etiquette that a Muslim should display before meeting God.

You cover your body to display your humility and modesty in front of God. Even though He created you and is aware of everything, you show the same respect that you would to God as you would show when meeting anyone else.

You pray during certain times of the day to keep a program of discipline for yourself. Your ego would distract you away from remembering God and tell you: "don't worry, pray later." However, with a strict, yet flexible, schedule you learn to make time for God always.

You face Makkah because it contains the Ka'bah, the first building dedicated to the worship of the one true God. This building was made by Prophet Ibrāhīm [Abraham] and his son Ismā'īl [Ishmael]. By facing it, you remind yourself, and everyone else, that you are among the true followers of Abraham.

Standing

Before you begin the prayer, you stand with full attention before God. Your head is slightly lowered out of respect.

Raising Hands

Before beginning the prayer, you remove all other thoughts, worries, and images from your mind. When you raise your hands near your head, you imagine that all other thoughts in your mind are being thrown behind you. Now your prayer has really begun.

Allāhu Akbar means that God is the greatest. Literally, it actually means 'God is greater'. He is greater and more important than anything else in your life. Remembering Him throughout prayer is greater and more beneficial than anything else you could be doing at the moment, and this is a reminder to yourself of that fact.

Standing for Recitation

Keeping your hands folded in front of anyone is a sign of respect and humility in front of that person. God is most deserving that you humble yourself in front of Him.

You say "I seek protection with God from the cursed Satan" before beginning the recitation of the Qur'ān. It purifies your ego and reminds you that you need God's assistance so you aren't distracted during your prayer. It also is a sign of humility since you admit that you don't have full control over your own thoughts, so you ask God to help you avoid the whispers of Satan, both in your prayer and in your life.

You say "In the name of God, the Most Kind and Merciful" to purify your intention and make your recitation of the Qur'an purely for the sake of God, so that you can receive His kindness and mercy.

You recite the Fātiḥah, the first and most comprehensive chapter of the Qur'an. It begins by praising God, who is the Lord and Master of everything in existence. Despite that, He is kind and merciful. He will be in control on the Day of Judgment, when all people will be held accountable as to how they lived their lives. Then you begin speaking directly to God, declaring that you would never worship anyone but Him and that you are in need of His help. Next, comes the most important part: the invocation. You ask God to guide you along the correct path that leads to Paradise, the way that he led you to Islam. Finding the right path is not enough, you must make sure to stay on the path and you must move forward, rather than backward, so you ask God for help. The path is further defined: that you want to follow the way of life that righteous people followed, not the way of life followed by people who deliberately reject-ed the truth or were misled along a wrong path.

You say "āmīn" which literally means "answer". You ask God to answer your prayer since you just asked Him to guide you on the straight path. It is an additional request and an emphasis that you really need God's guidance. It is also a source of optimism since you know that God an-swers prayers when they are done with sincerity.

You recite some verses of the Qur'an to reflect on the meaning and practice your memorization. One of the shortest, yet deepest chapters of the Qur'an is al-Ikhlās. In it, Prophet Muhammad was instructed by God to declare that God is one and eternal. He neither has children or parents. Nothing in this world can compare to God in any way because He is transcendent above all His creation.

Bowing

You humble your body before God by lowering it in a bow-ing position. This reminds you of your place in front of God.

You say "Glory be to my Lord, the great" manifesting your humility in front of God. The words are perfectly in line with the posture of bowing and you say 'my Lord' to make it more intimate and respectful. God may be the Lord of everyone but at this time you are only concerned with your relationship to Him.

Intermediate Standing

You stand up to take a break from bowing.

You say "God has heard the one who praised Him." You remind yourself that your prayer is not in vain and that God hears the prayer of everyone who sincerely praises Him.

You say "Our Lord, you are deserving of praise" Thereafter, you praise Him one more time to express your certainty about what you just said and prepare for the most important part of the prayer.

Prostration

This position is the most humbling experience where you put your face, which represents your honor, on the floor in front of God. It reminds you that God's guidance must remain above man's own inclinations and desires.

You say "Glory be to my Lord, the highest" manifesting your humility once again. However, this time, you contrast your lowly humble position with the lofty highness of God.

Intermediate Sitting

You sit up to take a break from prostrating.

Prostration #2

You prostrate once again, revealing the importance of this humble position in front of God.

Sitting

You sit in a comfortable and relaxing position after having stood for a while.

You say "Greetings, prayers, and all pure things ultimately belong to God. May the peace of God be with you, Prophet, as well as God's mercy and blessings. May the peace of God be with us and with all of God's righteous servants." All of the respectful greetings and praise that people give to idols, kings, and rulers actually belong to God, because He is deserving of them. The same is the case with all forms of prayer as well as any other pure action, since God is pure and only accepts that which is pure. You send peace on the Prophet because he is your guide chosen by God. You then send peace on yourself and on all other righteous people, praying that you become one of the righteous whom God is pleased with.

You say "I declare that no one deserves to be worshipped except God and I declare that Muhammad is His servant and messenger." This declaration brought you into Islam and you reaffirm it during every prayer. You reaffirm that nothing else in life is worth obeying except for God and that the only way to worship and obey Him properly is through the Messenger of God. You raise your right index finger while saying this to signify that God is one.

You say "God, bless Muhammad and his family, just as you have blessed Ibrāhīm and his family. You are the praiseworthy and glorious. God, favor Muhammad and his family, just as you have favored Ibrāhīm and his family. You are the praiseworthy and glorious." The messages of Prophet Muhammad and Ibrāhīm are directly linked, which is why you face the Ka'bah. You ask God to bless and give success to the last and final Prophet the same way that it Ibrāhīm and his descendants were blessed.

Finish the Prayer

You say "May the peace and mercy of God be with you." It is befitting to close the prayer with a call for peace and mercy because that is what Islam accomplishes. It brings peace in the life of the Muslim as well as in the society, so you turn your head in both directions while saying it so that it is directed towards everyone around you.

CONCLUSION

The bare minimum purpose of prayer is to take you away from your daily activities, for a few moments, to remember God. If you can accomplish at least this, the prayer will have some benefit. However, the ultimate goal should be to worship God with such concentration that it is as if you are standing directly in front of Him. Even though you cannot see God, He can see you. This may take a lifetime to achieve, but it is a goal that every Muslim should have in their life.

Recommended Sources

WEBSITES

http://www.welcometoislam.co

http://www.newmuslimsproject.net

http://www.quran.com

http://www.whyislam.org

ISLAMIC ITEMS

http://www.islamicbookstore.com

http://www.soundvision.com

VIDEOS

http://www.thedeenshow.com

http://www.halaltube.com

33726775R00033

Made in the USA
Lexington, KY
07 July 2014